# Grand Finales

*Desserts and Sweets*
*Flavored with Liqueurs,*
*Rums, and Brandies*

*Dick Taeuber*

BARRON'S

Woodbury, New York · London · Toronto · Sydney

*All inquiries should be addressed to:*
Barron's Educational Series, Inc.
113 Crossways Park Drive
Woodbury, New York 11797

*Library of Congress Catalog Card No. 82-11564*
International Standard Book No. 0-8120-5452-0

**Library of Congress Cataloging in Publication Data**

Taeuber, Dick 1933-
  Grand finales.

  Includes index.
  1. Desserts.   2. Cookery (Liquors)   I. Title.
TX773.T33 1982      641.8'6      82-11564
ISBN 0-8120-5452-0

**Credits**
*Photography:*
    Matthew Klein, color photographs
    Helen Feingold, food preparation
    Linda Cheverton, stylist
    All table settings by Tiffany & Co.
    Flowers by Howe Floral
Jacket and cover design: Milton Glaser, Inc.
Book design: Milton Glaser, Inc.
PRINTED IN THE UNITED STATES OF AMERICA
2  3  4  5  6      049   9  8  7  6  5  4  3  2

*Cover: Matching layers of liqueur – in a pousse-café and in a mousse cake, pages 36-37 and 207-11*
*Back cover: Amaretto Cheesecake, page 168*

# Contents

*To Richard, Susan, and Karen*
*in appreciation of friendship, support, and love*

# Preface

*G*rand Finales is for cooks who are careful and conscientious in their efforts, whether they have a great deal of experience or not. All too often cookbooks come across as requiring a lot of work, or the recipes seem overly complicated without adequate discussion. I have tried to avoid this, hoping to give you ideas and suggestions for making the desserts work well, plus instructions that are clear and easy to understand. Particularly, I've tried to keep in mind the hectic schedules most of us keep, whether we work full time at a job or spend our days managing a household and a growing family.

The theme of this book is experimentation and personal preference in flavorings. In many recipes there is a large range of liqueurs which might be used singly or in combinations. Choose the ones you like and/or the ones you have on hand, balanced with the tastes and flavors in the recipe you are making.

Remember also in your experimenting that the liqueurs are to serve as flavoring agents. As such, quality becomes important because better products tend to have more and stronger flavor; they are smoother and more dynamic as well. When you are making desserts for your family or friends, any serving of your dessert has only a small quantity of the liqueur, so be wary of sacrificing quality to save a little money.

This book came about because of a sense that liqueurs, rums, and brandies provide a very much underused flavoring for foods. There is no intent to increase the consumption of alcoholic beverages; indeed, if used in cooking — as are vanilla and other extracts, which have an alcohol base — the alcohol that is present will evaporate when heated or cooked and only the flavor will remain.

# *Acknowledgments*

To my mother, for engendering my confidence in my ability to cook and to experiment even as early as age 9 or 10; for suffering in silence through over-baked cookies and slanting cakes; for not telling me until some decades later what a disaster the kitchen was after, at age 12 with my 9-year-old brother helping, I had fixed a surprise full dinner featuring roast chicken and lemon meringue pie.

To Craig Claiborne, of the *New York Times,* who became intrigued with a cordial pie recipe with twenty flavor combinations and ran it in his Sunday August 3, 1975, column. From that first formal recognition came the expansion to well over two hundred variations, as are discussed in the mousse chapter. It also led to my expanded interest in the use of liqueurs as a flavoring agent in other desserts — and thus this book.

To a multitude of friends and colleagues, too numerous to mention individually, who enjoyed or suffered through the trials of many of the recipes. A few are specifically acknowledged throughout the book for their suggestions of recipes or concepts. Special thanks go to the members — gourmands one and all — of F-3 and the Gourmet Group, especially the GG Board, for their encouragement, support, and tasting.

To the food and beverage staff at the Hyatt Regency in Knoxville, Tennessee, for their reactions to the concept and the manuscript as both evolved. My son works there in food purchasing.

To Barron's for a willingness to challenge me to expand past the mousse/pie and present you with a full-range dessert book. Thanks also to everyone involved in the production aspects of the book, both those named in various places herein, as well as those who have worked anonymously.

Final, and special, thanks go to Carole Berglie for serving in the honored role of devil's advocate as well as applying her diligent editorial eye, in both roles making significant improvement in both the quality of the book and its convenience.

# Liqueurs, Rums, and Brandies

*Man is here at liberty to give to his liqueurs practically any shade of color he thinks best to attract the attention, raise the curiosity, and charm the eye; he also has at his command all the fruits of the earth from which to extract an almost unlimited variety of aromas and flavors, wherewith to please the most fastidious taste and flatter the most jaded palate.*

— *Andre Simon,* Wines and Spirits

*T*he multiplicity and diversity of liqueurs of the world sparkle in desserts. At the end of the meal, their variegated flavors can provide an infinity of desserts ranging from a simple, small glass of a single liqueur to a flaming Crêpes Suzette or Cherries Jubilee. One can pour a small amount of liqueur over fruit or ice cream, or blend it into the ice cream. A liqueur could replace the vanilla extract in many baked goods, be the major flavor in a cheesecake or a mousse, or provide the *coup de theatre* when you dim the lights and flambé your dessert at the table. Liqueur can be served simply with coffee, combined in a multilayered colorful pousse-café, or used in the sauce of Cherries Jubilee or Bananas Foster which is then flamed just before serving. Increasingly, professional chefs and amateur gourmets (those who cook conscientiously and carefully) use liqueurs to provide an innovative, extraordinary taste experience throughout the meal: as a flavorful ingredient in appetizers, entrées, side dishes, and — as is the focus of this book — to sparkle in desserts.

Cooking with liqueurs may be easier even than using other flavoring agents that may be more familiar. First, virtually every liqueur is sold in half-pints or even miniatures so you do not have to go to the extravagence of buying fifths or quarts. And then you could accompany the dessert with small cordial glasses of the same liqueur, and use up any leftovers that way. Second, the vintage of a liqueur is of relevance only at the time of bottling. Fruit liqueurs should not be aged; those made from the seeds, peels, or leaves of plants are frequently left in a cask for several years for the flavors to blend. But if made by one of the traditional processes — percolation, maceration, or distillation — once bottled the liqueurs are not improved by keeping, nor do they deteriorate except possibly over a period of years, unless abused in storage.

Regrettably, there is a catch in this last benefit. Some, presumably lesser, brands make liqueurs and cordials by adding sugar, extracts, and flavorings to a neutral spirit, usually grain alcohol or vodka. This approach is also promoted for the home manufacture of liqueurs. Made by this method, liqueurs have no degree of stabilization and thus should be consumed quickly.

# What is a Liqueur or a Cordial?

Most liqueurs or cordials—the terms generally are used interchangeably, although some use *liqueur* to refer to European products and *cordial* to American products—are produced by processing fruits or flavorful plant parts in spirits and then adding sugar. In fact, by U.S. law, liqueurs and cordials differ from all other spirits in that they must contain at least 2½ percent sugar or other sweetening agent. They may also have coloring added to make them more eye appealing. In the United States, a product labeled "brandy" must be a distillate obtained solely from the fermented juice, mash, or wine of the fruit involved. Fruit-flavored brandies must be made solely with a brandy base, have a minimum proof of 70, and have at least 2½ percent sugar by weight.

Liqueurs/cordials are produced by one of three general processes, whether they are based on an ancient, jealously guarded secret formula, are a simple, generic liqueur made by most cordial makers, or are a relatively new proprietary product. Those three processes—percolation, maceration, or distillation—may be used alone or in combination.

## PERCOLATION

This is the process many of us use to make coffee. Neutral or basic spirits are placed in the bottom of a large tank, with the flavoring agent such as fruit placed in a basketlike container at the top. The spirits are pumped from the bottom, sprayed over the flavoring agent, and then drip back to the spirit pool at the bottom. The process is continued until the desired flavor level is reached, or until there is no more flavor at the top.

## MACERATION

This is the process used in making tea. The flavoring agents are added to the base spirit, frequently brandy, and allowed to steep until the spirit has absorbed the essential flavors. The heavily flavored spirits are then distilled anew to produce the delicacy of flavor.

## DISTILLATION

This is the process one thinks of when we hear about moonshine and other home brews. For liqueurs, the leaves, fruit peels, seeds, and so forth are placed in the still, covered with a base alcoholic spirit, and then the mixture is distilled: that is, it is heated, the liquid vaporizes and the steam condenses. This process usually produces a high-proof, highly flavored spirit which is then adjusted to bottling proof by the addition of syrups or a thinner such as water.

The flavors of liqueurs are many and varied, and seem to be getting more so with every trip to the liquor store. Nonetheless, in a general sense liqueurs can be said to fall into five major categories, based on the flavor that dominates their taste: fruits, seeds, herbs, peels, and cremes. Fruits, peels, and cremes usually have a single dominant flavoring agent, and they are plainly labeled as cherry, raspberry, menthe, cacao, or curaçao (oranges). Seeds, herbs, roots, and flowers are usually a combination of any number, up to forty-eight or even more, though in the seed liqueurs a seed flavor such as anise usually dominates. Cremes are usually the sweetest of the liqueurs because of their high sugar content, which results in the creamlike consistency.

## SOME HISTORICAL BACKGROUND

Spirits of varying types are thoroughly intertwined with the recorded history of mann.* Homer related how one of Circe's attractions in luring Odysseus' men was a Pramnian wine. The Romans were said to not only have imbibed wine in large amounts, but also to have often cooked with wine, *and even fed wine* to the animals, birds, fish, or other creatures that they ate. Joan of Arc supposedly ate little other than a heavy soup, but is said to have customarily poured a quantity of wine into her bowl before filling it with soup. Since the alcohol would not have vaporized, as it does when cooked, this might explain her compelling voices which were not audible to others. The earliest known cookbooks dating to the late fifteenth century include recipes calling for wine as a flavor or cooking agent. In Colonial America, Caribbean rum, native corn whiskey, and apple brandy found their way into steaming mincemeat or pumpkin and fruit pies.

The Arabs are credited with being the first to distill, with the art rapidly adopted in the West where "chemists" used the process in their search for the secret to eternal life, for a "fountain of youth." Our ancestors thought of liqueurs as potent and effective medicines, good for "what ails one." Liqueurs were thought to ward off fevers and to possess healing properties. Even down through time to the more recent Hadacol and Tiger Balm, has mann had a curative, high-proof elixir.

Because of their healing properties, and because medicine in the Middle Ages was mainly in the hands of the religious orders in Europe, the theologians took control, and monks became the creators and producers of these magical spirits. To increase medicinal effect, or improve taste, or to have the "newest and most potent health elixir," almost any conceivable flavoring agent was tried: bark, leaves, nuts, beans, seeds, roots, flowers, juices, fruits, even metalic flakes or dust. The successful efforts can be said to have provided sufferers with the benefits of medicinal herbs such as caraway seeds, which are still used to soothe infant

*Following usage in Old English, *mann* will denote humankind, *man* will be gender specific.

is tired or has overeaten. *Cordial,* the interchangeable term for liqueur, has its derivation in the Latin *cor,* for heart, because of the early use of cordials as a heart stimulant.

Discussions of the origins of liqueurs usually focus on three specific liqueurs: the generic, or widely produced *goldwasser;* and the proprietary, meaning sufficiently complex formulas which have been protected — for example, *D.O.M. Benedictine* and *Chartreuse.*

Goldwasser, on the bottle of one maker, is said to have been created in a "Benedict Bros. Monastery built in 733 AD." More conventionally it is credited to a Spanish-born chemist, Arnaud de Villeneuve, and dates to the late thirteenth century, although maybe his home monastery was built in 733 AD. To avoid being caught up by the terrors of the Inquisition, he created a "new, improved" health elixir for the ailing Pope by adding caraway for digestion, anise for taste, plus other herbs and spices for various subsidiary potential benefits. As his special, ultimate ingredient, he added tiny gold flakes which are still viewed as protection against various unspecified diseases. Fortunately the Holy Father recovered, and a liqueur was born. Even today this widely made, crystal-clear liqueur is considered a digestif throughout much of Europe. Its tiny flakes of gold leaf are so light that they cannot be felt on the tongue, but they create a spectacular effect when the bottle is shaken.

D.O.M. Benedictine is doubtless the oldest of the surviving proprietary liqueurs, dating back to 1510. To quickly clarify, the D.O.M. has always stood for the Latin *Deo optimo maximo,* or "To God, most good, most great." It is credited to a Benedictine monk, Bernardo Vincelli, who wanted a better health elixir with improved medicinal and restorative powers for the tired or sick monks. Almost three centuries later, the ravages of the French Revolution ultimately reached the Benedictine Abbey in Fécamp, Normandy, with the consequence that D.O.M. Benedictine vanished from the marketplace for some seventy years. Scholar A. Le Grand found a copy of the formula among a collection of manuscripts and records during his research in 1863. Recognizing his "find," he began the manufacture of Benedictine on a secular and commercial basis, but still in Fécamp where there is now a museum beside the plant, one which is well worth seeing. There is no longer any connection with any religious order, but the formula still is well protected. Supposedly, only three people at any one time know the complete formula. Made on a fine cognac base and aged for four years before bottling, its flavor is claimed to derive from a mixture of twenty-seven herbs, plants, and peels which include angelica root, aloe, arnica, cardamom, coriander, melissa, myrrh, hyssop, nutmeg, mace, artemisia, pine cone, vanilla, maidenhair fern, cinnamon, saffron, and grain seeds.

Chartreuse seems to be the oldest proprietary liqueur continuously made by the same organization: the Carthusian Fathers. The original formula (which seems a more appropriate term than *recipe*) was given to the Carthusian Fathers of the Convent of the Grande Chartreuse at Grenoble sometime before 1610 by

the Maréchal d'Estrées. The formula was refined or improved in the middle of the eighteenth century by one of the monks, Brother Jérôme Maubec. Initially an elixir reserved for the holy brethren, word of its "powers" gradually spread, and the demand was such that production had to be increased, and the Fathers had to produce for an expanding commercial market.

As contrasted with the fates of Benedictine, the monastery at Chartreuse was largely spared the ravages of the French Revolution. Bureaucracy played its games, however, and the formula was requisitioned by the civil authorities. When it turned up in the Ministry of Secret Remedies in 1810, its potential was not recognized, and the minister returned it to the fathers with the word *refused* written across the parchment. They were not totally to escape turmoil in France, for in the early part of this century a law was passed there outlawing religious orders. The fathers fled their monastery and sought sanctuary in Tarragona, Spain. Civil authorities auctioned off the Chartreuse trademark and the monastery. In Tarragona, the production of Chartreuse was begun anew under the label *"Liqueur Fabriquée à Tarragona par les Père Chartreux"* using the same secret formula building on a brandy base. The Frenchmen who acquired the trademark put on the market a product labeled Chartreuse, of quite different quality, which induced a need among sophisticated buyers to check the labels carefully. After World War II, the order was allowed to return to Grenoble, near the French Alps, and now most of the production of Chartreuse occurs there under the supervision of four monks. They, and a fifth monk who supervises the production in Tarragona (which is operated about six weeks a year), are the only ones who know the total formula.

Chartreuse is known to have a brandy base, but speculation on the number of herbs, roots, seeds, and spices ranges up as high as 130, with the specific ingredients and proportions known only to the five monks. It is produced in three varieties: green which is drier and more aromatic at 110 proof; yellow which is sweetened with honey at 86 proof; and a V.E.P., 108 proof, which is aged for fifteen years, produced in very limited quantities for special occasions only, and not exported.

Proeflakaalen, the Dutch liqueur-tasting rooms, also date to the sixteenth century. During this period, Holland was entering her golden age of prosperity and influence. To compete with the French imports, they developed their own approach to liqueurs based on grain alcohols, rather than fruit-based products. To the spirits distilled from grain mash were added various flavoring agents, and the range of products offered the customers in the tasting rooms was gradually expanded. Amsterdam's first tasting room, 't Lootsje, was opened by Lucas Bols in 1575, and it operated continuously until 1967 when the tasting shop finally had to be moved to larger, somewhat more modern quarters. A ritual of the tasting process, from the earliest days, is for the glass to be served full-to-the-brim, requiring the taster to bend at the waist, in a kind of bow that is called "doing honor to the drink."

Not content to limit himself to the production of simple grain spirits, Bols took to experimenting with adding various spices, fruits, seeds, and nuts to enhance the flavor of his products, and to have a variety of products to offer his customers. He introduced the use of anise as a flavoring in anisette, used Dutch-grown caraway seeds as the basis for kümmel, and refined a previously unknown orange, brought to Holland from the Dutch West Indian colony of Curaçao, to create the essence for triple sec.

Bols clientele steadily expanded, and came to include Rembrandt, who came regularly for his *borreltje* ("little drink"). Even Peter the Great stopped by to get recipes to take home to Russia. Over the centuries the Bols line has expanded to more than one hundred different types of spirits and liqueurs, based on the original flavoring agents as well as coffee, chocolate, whiskey, eggs, spices from Spain and the Far East, myrrh from Iraq, orange-tree bark from the Netherlands Antilles, and angelica from the mountains of central Europe, among others.

Those early liqueurs were valued, supposedly, for their therapeutic properties of healing and soothing, and also as aphrodisiacs. In fact, they were often referred to as liqueurs of the heart, even though initially everyone's products tended to be harsh and medicinal. Another early Dutch liqueur giant, Johs. de Kuyper, who was on the scene somewhat after Bols, applied himself to the arts of the palate rather than the palette. This new concept in liqueurs began the movement toward elixirs which were smooth and carefully formulated to titillate the nose and the tongue—that is, cordials to be enjoyed.

# *Brandewijn*

Brandy came about from the refinement and concentration of the original winelike distillate drunk throughout most of known history. In medieval days, wine from the grapes of France was exported widely throughout the rest of western Europe. Duties were levied on bulk, so the winegrowers thought to save money by distilling—or burning—their wine. The Dutch called this concentrate *brandewijn*, or burned wine. This promptly was shortened to *brandy*, now a universally understood word.

Brandy usually is interpreted to mean the liquor distilled from the fermented juices of ripe grapes, but as will be discussed later, various other fruits may also provide a basis for brandy. The best brandies are usually a blend of several separately processed brandies to produce a smoother, fuller-flavored product. Also, many brandy winegrowers are quite small, and may begin the two-step distillation themselves, before they sell to the major houses for further processing and blending prior to bottling. The finest grape brandies today are those bearing the designation *cognac*, yet—strangely enough—the wines from which

cognac is made are sour, brakish, and distinctly unpalatable. It is only after they have been distilled and aged that they acquire the smoothness, the bouquet, and the character that makes them so distinctive and pleasurable.

As with liqueurs, one can not talk about vintage. Wine is a living thing, which reaches a peak and then begins a downhill slide because it is not distilled. The heat of distillation destroys all microorganisms, so that the only changes which take place come from the interaction of the brandy and the wood of the aging cask, with no further change once it is in the bottle. Since wood is porous, aging brandy can evaporate, albeit quite slowly. Given the length of time that the finer brandies are aged, to avoid the disagreeable surprise of opening a cask many years later only to find its contents substantially depleted, care is taken to add some of each year's distillate to the aging casks already in use. Once the brandy is in the bottle, after its wooden cask aging, it can be kept around for years, with the bottle getting dustier and dustier, making absolutely no difference in the brandy.

*Eau-de-vie* (or the plural, *eaux*), the dry, strong fruit brandies from the nongrape areas of Switzerland, Italy, and France, are another major surviving set of products of the sixteenth century. They may date back to the fourteenth century or even earlier, for initially, and for long periods, they were modest, homemade spirits. Unlike cognac and other brandies, these have been aged in crockery, not in wood, so there is nothing to cushion their harshness or to tame their aroma. At 90 to 100 proof, they are to be sipped and savored.

The *eaux-de-vie* are also called *alcools blanc* by the French because they are close to colorless, with a warm, fruity aroma and a distinct taste of their fruit. Of the fruit brandies, kirsch or kirschwasser is made from black cherries; framboise is made from wild, small black raspberries from the Vosges; apricot is from Austro-Hungarian apricots; poire william is made from Swiss William pears, and occasionally is sold with a whole pear in the bottle (which contributes little and occupies space); mirabelle is made from primarily yellow plums; and quetsch is made from primarily blue plums. These should be served chilled, or in a chilled glass, so that subsequent warming releases their beautiful aroma. Try large glasses and small pourings, followed by a gentle swirling of the *eau-de-vie* so that the clear, clean aroma becomes deeper and more penetrating, and the taste is enhanced. Drinking an *eau-de-vie* is uncannily like biting on fresh-picked fruit, if fully savored. They are rich but rarely sweeter than medium dry,* for the stones are mashed along with the flesh of the fruit; those stones are responsible for the slightly bitter almond flavor of these brandies, in addition to cutting the sweetness.

*"dry," when referring to alcoholic products, refers not to an absence of wetness, but to the degree of sweetness; that is, a drier wine or liqueur is one that is less sweet.

# Yo, Ho, Ho and a Bottle of...

Rum is the drink of romantics, the favorite of adventurers and pirates. It is another product of the early sixteenth century, a by-product of the introduction of sugarcane into the Caribbean by Columbus on one of his later voyages. To produce sugar, the cane is crushed and mangled between rollers to extract a juice which is reduced to a concentrated syrup by boiling. Most of the sugar is crystallized out of the concentrated juice of the cane, about 5 percent remains in the heavy, dark syrup residue which is molasses. When sufficient residue is on hand, the mixture is fermented, distilled, redistilled, aged, filtered, colored, flavored, and cut to bottling strength. (One can imagine the early distiller-chemist bemoaning the absence of any grape or other fruit juice from which to produce the more familiar wines of his homeland, then happening upon this sugar-rich syrup residue, and the light of inspiration glowing ever stronger.)

In its earliest forms, rumbullion, shortened to rum, was little more than a high-strength firewater. As experience, sophistication, and demand produced better stills and the idea of aging rum in casks, the smooth drink we know today began to develop. Its popularity became so great that those railing against alcoholic beverages of any nature used the phrase *demon rum.* Another name for rum came from its being dispensed in a daily ration to troops on the line or sailors at sea: that term is *grog*, and the name came from the belief of a British Admiral that rum had medicinal properties (as were assigned all liqueurs in their early days), especially as a precaution against scurvy. Admiral Edward Vernon (the namesake of George Washington's estate, Mount Vernon) is the one who initially insisted that his men have a daily ration of water and rum; although the water probably counteracted any positive effect of the rum. The Admiral was known as "Old Grog" because he wore a shabby coat made of grogram, a fabric woven from silk and wool.

Rums today are a familiar part of any liquor store stock. The white, silver, or platinum rums generally have a delicate, elusive, subdued flavor which blends well and is thus an excellent cocktail base, an extender of other flavors. The dark rums, associated with Jamaica and other islands, have a pungent, all-pervasive bouquet that can stand up to another flavor. The dark rums are preferred for long drinks where the flavor has to last, and for use in small amounts to impart a rum flavor in cooking.

Rums are made wherever sugar is produced, but owing to the climate or soil or water or something, only those made in and around the Caribbean are of sufficient quality to produce for export. The multiplicity of exported rums fall into three main types: the light-bodied rums of Cuba; the heavy-bodied rums of Jamaica and Damerara; and the medium or "in-between" rums ranging from Barbados and New England, which are close to the heaviness of the Jamaicans, to the Virgin Islands and Mexican rums and on to those Puerto Rican rums that approach the Cuban but still differ because of water and soil differences.

# A Brief Glossary of Terms and Names

## LIQUEURS

**ABSINTHE:** a light, yellow-green high-proof spirit with a pronounced anise or licorice aroma. The original aromatic — oils of wormwood — is banned in the United States and many other countries because it is said to be habit-forming, hallucinogenic, and to result in insanity and sterility. The available sweeter and lower-proof substitute is Pernod, named after the maker of absinthe. 68 proof, proprietary.

**ADVOKAAT:** a mixture of egg yolks, sugar, and brandy, creamy thick with an eggnog flavor. 30 proof, generic.

**AMARETTO:** a sweet, pleasing almond-flavored liqueur created from the pits of apricots, steeped in acquavite, a fusion of alcohol, and accented with Madagascan vanilla by some manufacturers. The original Amaretto di Saronno, from Saronno, Italy, dates back to the mid-sixteenth century. 48 to 56 proof, generic.

**ANISETTE:** a clear, sweet, mild aromatic liqueur made from aniseeds and aromatic herbs such as bitter almonds, coriander, etc. Sold as a clean, crisp red and a lively white. 50 to 60 proof, generic.

**BÄRENJÄGER:** a honey-based liqueur produced in Bavaria. 70 proof, proprietary.

**D.O.M. BENEDICTINE:** made from an ancient formula using herbs and plants cultivated, mostly, near the Benedictine Abbey in Fécamp, Normandy, although it has been made privately for over 100 years. This never-duplicated product is discussed on page 4. 86 proof, proprietary.

**B & B LIQUEUR D.O.M.:** an equal-part blend of D.O.M. Benedictine and drier cognac, offered in response to growing indications that many Benedictine drinkers were doing their own mixing. 80 proof, proprietary.

**CARAMELLA:** a blending of the tastes of caramel and vanilla. 54 proof, proprietary.

**CHAMBORD LIQUEUR ROYAL DE FRANCE:** dating from the time of Louis XIV, it is made from small black raspberries and other fruits and herbs combined with honey. 33 proof, proprietary.

**CHARTREUSE:** said to contain as many as 130 herbs and spices, this monastery-produced product is offered in green at 110 proof and yellow at 86 proof (see pages 4-5), proprietary.

**CHERI-SUISSE:** from Switzerland with a flavor based on semisweet chocolate enhanced with the subtle flavor of fine cherries. 60 proof, proprietary.

**CHOCLAIR:** a flavor based on a fine chocolate with a hint of coconut. 54 proof, proprietary.

**CHOCOLATE BANANA/CHERRY/MINT/RASPBERRY:** a series of rich, creamy cordials blending cocoa-chocolate, vanilla, and other flavors. 54 proof, generic.

**COCONUT:** a rich, fruity liqueur based on coconuts processed quickly after harvest. 60 proof, generic.

**COCORIBE LIQUEUR:** a combination of coconut, other flavors, and light Virgin Island rum. 60 proof, proprietary.

**COFFEE:** a variety of liqueurs based on the sweetened essences of coffees. (They are usually sold under a proprietary label such as Kahlua, Pasha, or Tia Maria.) 50 to 70 proof, generic.

**COINTREAU:** this colorless liqueur, with the flavor of carefully selected sweet and bitter Mediterranean and tropical orange peels and a cognac base, is the finest of the triple secs. Originally Cointreau referred to a full line of liqueurs, but now the name refers to the orange triple sec only; the other products being marketed under the Regnier label. 80 proof, proprietary.

**CORDIAL MÉDOC:** a blend of rare old brandies, orange curaçao, crème de cacao, champagne cognac, and claret from the Médoc wine district in France. 80 proof, proprietary.

**CRANBERRY LIQUEUR:** tart, tangy with the taste of fresh, ripe cranberries. 40 proof, generic.

**CRÈME D'ANANA:** made from fresh pineapple, brandy, and a bit of vanilla. Generic.

**CRÈME DE BANANA:** made from fresh, ripe bananas. 50 to 60 proof, generic.

**CRÈME DE CACAO:** made from cacao beans, vanilla beans, and a hint of spices, this comes in a brown, deep chocolate flavor version and a white version whose chocolate flavor is less intense and is colorless. *Chouao* on the label implies that the cacao beans are from the Chouao region of Venezuela, considered the finest cacao beans. 54 to 60 proof, generic.

**CRÈME DE CASSIS:** made from black currants grown principally around Dijon, France. 40 proof, generic. (A proprietary Double Crème de Cassis has a much stronger flavor.)

**CRÈME DE MENTHE:** a distillate of several varieties of mint, principally peppermint, which is sold in green, gold, and white (clear) versions. 60 proof, generic.

**CRÈME DE NOYAUX:** made from apricot and peach pits to produce a rich, nutty almond taste with a pink color, which is distinct from amaretto. 50 to 60 proof, generic.

**CURAÇAO:** made from the peels of the small, green, bitter oranges grown in the Dutch West Indies including the island of Curaçao, along with other orange peels, spices, rum, port wine, sugar, and brandy. Sold in orange and blue versions, with the blue generally slightly lower in proof. Like triple sec but slightly sweeter, somewhat lower in proof, and with a more subtle orange flavor. 54 to 80 proof, generic.

**DRAMBUIE:** produced in Scotland by flavoring old Scotch whiskey with heather honey and a small hint of a few herbs and spices; dates back to 1745. 80 proof, proprietary.

**DROSTE BITTERSWEET CHOCOLATE LIQUEUR:** made in Holland, slightly dry with a pronounced flavor of bittersweet chocolate. 54 proof, proprietary.

**FRAISE DE BOIS:** a liqueur deriving its fragrant taste and flavor from small wild strawberries. 40 to 50 proof, generic.

**FRAMBOISE:** the raspberry *eau-de-vie*, a raspberry brandy under U.S. definition. 86 to 100 proof, generic.

**FRANGELICO:** said to date back some 300 years, this Italian liqueur is flavored with wild hazelnuts blended with berries and herbs. 56 proof, proprietary.

**GINGER-FLAVORED BRANDY:** grape brandy with the pungent flavor and aroma of gingerroot, with other select aromatics. 70 proof, generic.

**GOLDWASSER:** a crystal-clear liqueur containing tiny flakes of gold leaf. Made from spices, figs, lemon peel, and herbs in a brandy base (see page 4). 50 proof, generic.

**GRAND MARNIER:** an orange-flavored liqueur made from the distillate of the peel of bitter Curaçao oranges and blended with fine champagne cognac to produce a rare, distinctive flavor and bouquet. 80 proof, proprietary.

**GREENSLEEVES:** one of an increasing set of cream liqueurs which have been made possible by new technology that allows longer, unrefrigerated shelf life, even when opened. Made in England with a mint and chocolate flavor in a brandy base. 34 proof, proprietary.

**IRISH CREAM LIQUEUR:** a cream liqueur (see above) based on Irish whiskey. Various brands may have other flavorings added in slight amounts. 34 proof, with each of the various brands proprietary and somewhat distinctive.

**IRISH MIST:** a blend of four Irish whiskeys, heather honey, clover, and the essence of a dozen herbs. 80 proof, proprietary.

**IZARRA:** a Basque liqueur with an Armagnac base and a touch of mimosa honey, with the green containing forty-eight herbs and spices at 100 proof, the yellow with thirty-two herbs and spices at 86 proof. Proprietary.

**KAHLÚA:** a Mexican coffee liqueur made on a brandy base with flavor from the choicest coffee beans, cocoa beans, and vanilla. 63 proof, proprietary.

**KIRSCHWASSER OR KIRSCH**: the black cherry *eau-de-vie*, a cherry brandy under U.S. definition. 90 to 100 proof, generic.

**KÜMMEL**: one of the earliest grain-based spirit liqueurs, flavored with caraway and a hint of anise and other herbs including cumin and coriander. 70 to 82 proof, generic.

**LEMONIER/LEMONIQUE**: liqueurs with flavors based on lemon peels which are sweet, tart, and decidedly lemon in color. 74 proof, each is proprietary.

**LIQUORE GALLIANO**: a spicy, golden Italian liqueur with a brandy base and a selection of seeds, herbs, and spices. Named after the Italian Major, Guiseppe Galliano. 80 proof, proprietary.

**LIQUORE STREGA**: the other major Italian *liqueur de dessert* is rich, fragrant, and golden with its flavor derived from a combination of more than seventy herbs. 80 proof, proprietary.

**MANDARINE/MANDARINE NAPOLEON/MANDARINETTE**: a liqueur made from mandarin oranges (tangerines, the French word for which is *mandarine*) and brandy. The latter two are proprietary variations. 80 proof, generic.

**MARASCHINO**: an aromatic white liqueur made from the crushed pulp and pits of marasca cherries grown in the Dalmatia district on the west coast of the Adriatic Sea. The crushed pits provide the trace of almond flavor. 60 to 78 proof, generic.

**MIDORI**: a Japanese liqueur with the light, refreshing taste of fresh honeydew melon. 46 proof, proprietary.

**MIRABELLE**: the yellow-plum *eau-de-vie*, a plum brandy under U.S. definition. 82 to 86 proof, generic.

**NASSAU ROYALE**: from the Bahamas, a liqueur whose flavor comes from a blend of over twenty-two herbs and spices, and a hint of vanilla. 67 proof, proprietary.

**OUZO**: a sweet, white Greek liqueur with a pronounced licoricelike anise flavor. 92 proof, generic.

**PARFAIT AMOUR:** an exotic French liqueur with a brandy base flavored with flowers, oranges, lemons, and assorted herbs. 58 proof, generic.

**PEPPERMINT SCHNAPPS:** minty, predominantly peppermint, but with less sugar than crème de menthe. 60 proof, generic. (Schnapps, originally synonymous with the peppermint taste, now is being sold with a variety of flavors including ginger, spearmint, and cinnamon.)

**PETER HEERING:** formerly marketed as Cherry Heering, its flavor comes from fresh, ripe Danish cherries on a brandy base. Said to be Denmark's national liqueur. 49 proof, proprietary.

**POIRE (PEAR) WILLIAM:** the pear *eau-de-vie,* a pear brandy under U.S. definition. 90 to 100 proof, generic.

**PRALINE LIQUEUR:** a pecan and vanilla flavor deriving from the original New Orleans praline confection. 40 proof, proprietary.

**QUETSCH:** the blue-plum *eau-de-vie,* a plum brandy under U.S. definition. 82 to 86 proof, proprietary.

**SABRA:** an Israeli liqueur with flavor derived from tangy Jaffa oranges and fine chocolate. 60 proof, proprietary.

**SLOE GIN:** not a gin, but a liqueur whose flavor comes from the sloeberry, a wild plum from France. 42 to 60 proof, generic.

**SOUTHERN COMFORT:** bourbon whiskey with a moderate quantity of peach liqueur and freshly peeled and pitted peaches added. The fruit and the liqueur help mellow the robust body of the bourbon. 100 proof, proprietary.

**STRAWBERRY/WILD STRAWBERRY LIQUEUR:** a brandy base with the full, fruity flavor of fresh strawberries. See also Fraise de Bois. 40 to 50 proof, generic.

**TIA MARIA:** a 200-year-old formula based on an essence of Jamaican Blue Mountain coffee (said to be the

world's finest), blended with rare and delicate spices. 63 proof, proprietary.

**TRIPLE SEC:** similar to curaçao, but colorless, drier (less sweet), and higher in proof. Made from the peels of the same tangy, bittersweet green oranges as curaçao. 60 to 80 proof, generic.

**VANDERMINT:** the product of a Dutch family firm that has been making liqueurs since the sixteenth century, its flavor is fine Dutch chocolate with a touch of mint. 60 proof, proprietary.

**WILD TURKEY LIQUEUR:** to a fully aged bourbon base are added herbs, spices, and other natural flavorings. 80 proof, proprietary.

## BRANDIES

**APPLE BRANDY:** originally a local product of the province of Normandy, which had apples rather than grapes. The finest apple brandy is the Normandy-produced calvados. Distilled from apple cider, in this country it is usually known as applejack.

**ARMAGNAC:** produced in Gers, in the Basque region of France. Armagnac is often bottled straight, as contrasted to cognac, which is always blended. Armagnac matures rapidly, and is fine up to about twenty years of age at bottling.

**COGNAC:** the finest of the brandies, distilled from grapes grown in the Charente district of France, the principal city of which is Cognac. Only brandy from this district may properly, and legally, carry the designation *cognac.* Cognac is usually aged for twenty years or more in barrels made from nearby Limousin oak trees.

**EAU-DE-VIE:** See page 7 for a full discussion of these elegant fruit brandies.

**FRUIT BRANDIES:** as often mentioned, brandy may be made from the fermented juice of many fruits, not just grapes. The U.S. liquor laws require that if any sweetening is added, the product must be called a liqueur and not a brandy. Thus you will see on store shelves many bottles labeled "_____-Flavored Brandy" or "_____Liqueur" or "_____Cordial."

**RUMS**

**BARBADOS RUMS:** brandy-type rum, with clear flavor slightly heavier than Cuban and Puerto Rican rums.

**CUBAN RUMS:** especially the white label, have only a faint, elusive flavor which is unequaled in blends with almost any other liquor, liqueur, fruit syrup, or fruit juice.

**DEMERARA RUMS:** from Guiana, these are similar to the dark Jamaicans. They have a dry, burned, aromatic, pungent flavor and frequently are bottled as strong as 160 proof.

**HABANERO RUMS:** from Mexico, these are very light, mild-flavored; aged in Spanish sherry casks.

**HAITIAN RUMS:** delightful brandy-type rums well suited to tall drinks or being drunk straight.

**JAMAICAN RUMS:** the light, amber, and dark are all strong and pungent in flavor. A flavor that refuses to be subdued or tamed, they blend nicely with all fruit flavors and many liqueurs. They are better for long drinks, and in cooking where the flavor wants to stand up to the cooking and to other flavors.

**MARTINIQUE RUMS:** similar to Jamaican rums, they are heavy and often have a faint, dry burned flavor of the Demeraras. Rums made in Martinique may be shipped in bulk to France, aged further and bottled there, and reshipped as French rum.

**NEW ENGLAND RUMS:** from an industry that dates back to Colonial days, these rums are strong enough to warm the men of the fishing fleets in the North Atlantic.

**NEWFOUNDLAND RUMS:** the celebrated Screech de Terre-Neuve is produced in Jamaica and re-bottled in Newfoundland, for the fishing fleets and others needing warmth against the North Atlantic cold.

**PUERTO RICAN RUMS:** distilled in a manner similar to that used for the Cuban rums, but in a different location with different water. They are light bodied and sweet flavored. The gold-label rums are drier and more flavorful than the white-label rums.

**VIRGIN ISLANDS RUMS:** different — neither light nor heavy — with their own molasses flavor.

## Once Over Lightly:
# Techniques and Ingredients

*T*his chapter is for you to read *once over lightly*, and also to have available for reference. While working on this book, I found that procedural questions arose which had to be answered, or I discovered answers before I was aware of the questions. Use salted or unsalted butter? What can I do with leftover egg whites? At what temperature does chocolate melt? What is Dutch-process cocoa, and must I ask friends in Amsterdam to send me some? Should I use farm-fresh eggs to make my soufflé even better? How does one substitute honey for sugar? How should I whip cream to get it the fluffiest?

The recipes in the book generally **serve six**, but does the number of servings really mean much with desserts? At parties I have offered a choice of two of my cordial pies, which have been described as serving as few as six, but most guests then want a small slice of each. Some may prefer just one, wanting one-eighth of the pie, which I would call a normal serving, and others ask for a half or a third of that "normal" serving. Another consideration on serving quantity: are you serving the dessert as but the grand finale to a full meal, or as a major portion of your food offerings for your guests?

Although this is not a diet book, you can reduce the caloric content of some of the recipes if that is of concern. For instance, although sugar which is to be cooked in a custard or a cake is important to the chemistry of the process, if it is added merely for sweetening, you can reduce it at your own preference. In the Cordial Mousse recipe, the sugar cooked with the gelatin mixture should be left at ⅓ cup (70 g), but the sugar beaten into the egg whites could be reduced. Sugar in cake batter is necessary to allow the batter to rise properly and yield a cake which is light and moist, but you may be able to reduce the amount used in the frosting. Omit or use very simple garnishes; use a glaze rather than a full frosting for a cake; or pass the whipped cream in a separate dish for self-service, rather than topping each serving. Or offer those who are calorie-conscientious a smaller serving.

The recipes in this book have measurements expressed in U.S. conventional and metric measures. have given the metric measures as a conversion from the conventional, with only a small amount of rounding off to centiliters or 5-gram units for the most part.

# Baking and Baking Pans

Baking pans for cakes should be greased with a light coating over the entire inside surface of the pan, and then dusted with flour, as a general rule. Any excess flour (flour that is not sticking to the butter) should be tapped out by inverting the pan and rapping the rim on the edge of the sink or on a counter. Butter is generally preferred, but the greasing can be done with vegetable shortening.

If you have any doubts about removing the cake from the pan, bake on parchment paper or, especially for fragile cakes, on waxed paper. Grease the inside of the pan, place the paper round in the bottom, grease the top of the paper, and then dust the whole inside with flour. Brown wrapping paper can be used instead of parchment paper if it is not recycled paper. The chemicals required for the recycling process may impart strange flavors to your baking.

You can approximate a commercial oven by placing a baking sheet on an oven rack, providing the solid-shelf effect. You must preheat the baking sheet/shelf, and use only the one rack/shelf in your oven, otherwise the heat distribution will be spoiled. The case for this approach is probably strongest when baking soufflés, since the wire rack does not provide strictly even heat to the bottom of the soufflé or other mold.

Do not cram your oven full nor overfill a baking sheet, not so much for obvious reasons of expansion, but because moist-batter items that are too close will steam as well as bake and may become soggy.

Cool heavy cakes outside of their pans; light ones should remain in their pans. Brownies and other bars should be cooled in their pans.

# Saucepans

When cooking custards, gelatin mixtures, and so forth, there is often a requirement to bring the mixture to a given temperature and no further. Use a thin-walled saucepan; do not use a cast-iron or other heavy saucepan for such cooking. After you heat to the desired point, you want to stop the cooking process. Stirring for a minute or so aids the stopping, but the arresting of the cooking is much easier if the pan is not retaining heat. Note also that you should not set the pan back down on an electric burner for, unlike gas, electric burners will still be hot for some time after you turn off the heat.

# *Measuring Ingredients*

It is better to measure ingredients until you have a feel for the recipe, and the extent to which you can vary the quantity of any of the ingredients. Certainly if you are baking rather than cooking, precise measurements are more important.

With a seasoning or a flavoring agent, the amount used can be a matter of personal taste, but remember that it is relatively easy to add more flavor, spice, salt, or whatever but can be difficult to cut or dilute such a taste when too strong.

When measuring solid fats, peanut butter, and so forth, be sure to press down to eliminate or prevent air bubbles.

Flour, sugar, and similar large dry-measure ingredients can be measured by scooping out an overfull measure of the ingredient, and then using a straight edge to smooth the top of the measuring cup or spoon.

# *Beating or Mixing*

Mixing operations include beating, blending, creaming, cutting, folding, stirring, and whipping; each has important differences. For any of these operations, if you are using an electric mixer or blender, at intervals you should use a spatula to scrape down the sides of the mixing container in order to keep all the batter in the path of the beaters or blades. Depending on the fit of the beaters to the bottom of the container, you may also need to scrape the bottom of the bowl so that no batter — or egg whites or cream, or other ingredient — escapes the mixing operation. Re-read your mixer's instruction book for beating procedures and suggestions. If you have a light-duty (that is, a hand-held) mixer, most indicated mixings will take longer.

**BEATING:** an over-and-over motion to achieve a thorough mixing of the ingredients and usually to incorporate some air into the batter.

**BLENDING:** a gentle stirring, primarily to mix the ingredients. If you are blending dry and wet ingredients, it is best to add them alternately, in parts, beginning and ending with dry ingredients. The usual procedure is to add the dry ingredients in thirds, the wet in halves.

**CUTTING**:  generally a process to cut fat into flour using a special pastry blender or two knives. With the help of the coating action of the dry ingredients, the fat is cut into very fine particles.

**CREAMING**:  a process applied to butter — or another fat or cream cheese — to make it light and creamy. Frequently sugar is also creamed with the butter before other ingredients are beaten in to make the batter. To cream butter, or cream cheese, you want the butter softened, but not melted.

*By hand:* using a wooden spoon, mash, rub, and beat the butter against the sides of the bowl until the butter is light and uniformly creamy. At that point add the sugar, or whatever is called for, and repeat the combination of beating and stirring to get the mixture as light as possible.

*By mixer:* creaming can be done with an electric mixer, but it is easy only if you have a mixer with a pastry paddle. If you are using the conventional beaters, realize that you will have to stop frequently and scrape or push the mixture from the beaters.

**FOLDING**:  a gentle process for mixing a light, generally very airy ingredient such as whipped cream or beaten egg whites into a heavier ingredient such as a batter. The idea is to blend the two ingredients with a minimum loss of the air that has been beaten into the lighter one: a crucial aspect of fixing a soufflé. If the heavier batter is thicker than a light cream in consistency, then you should "lighten" the batter by stirring about ¼ to ⅓ of the airy ingredient into the batter. To fold, place the airy ingredient — say the beaten egg whites — on top of the lightened batter. Using a large spatula or a flat whisk, cut straight down through to the bottom of the bowl, rotate the spatula, and "scoop" so that some of the batter is laid over a portion of the whites. Rapidly repeat the process, rotating the bowl and acting gently, until all of the egg whites have been incorporated into the base mixture. Do a minimum of folding, so that you do not disrupt the potential rising of the dessert.

**STIRRING**:  a gentle circular motion, around and around the mixing bowl, working in a horizontal sense, not the vertical or up-and-down of beating.

**WHIPPING**:  a vigorous, rapid beating operation usually to incorporate air into an ingredient or batter. Purists would claim that the only proper tool for whipping is a balloon whisk, but a hand beater or an electric mixer can be used. For egg whites or whipping cream, a blender has action which is too fast and too vigorous. The verdict is out on whipping egg whites or cream in a food processor. In general neither ingredient gets as much air as might be desired, so the food processor should be used only as a last resort. And always note your recipe, and whip the ingredient only to the stage of stiffness called for by the recipe or the usage.

# Some Tips on Techniques

**COATING THE SPOON**

Cook until the mixture "coats the spoon" is an oft-used recipe phrase. The most frequent interpretation involves the use of a wooden spoon for stirring. To make the test, remove the spoon from the mixture being heated and stirred; some of the sauce or batter should cling to the spoon. Lick your finger, and then run that finger down the center of either side of the spoon. There should remain a clear spacing with the sauce, batter or custard coating either side.

Another test for this stage of doneness is that the mixture has reached a temperature of 170-180°F (75-80°C) as measured on a candy thermometer.

When the custard, or gelatin mixture, or whatever, has reached this state, you want to stop the cooking process quickly. Remove the pan from the heat, and stir the contents for a minute or so to stop the cooking. Or arrest the heating by pouring the mixture into a cold bowl. If you allow the mixture to continue cooking, either directly or from retained heat in the saucepan, the mixture might curdle.

**CLARIFYING BUTTER**

Clarifying is a process to remove the solid matter from butter, preferably unsalted butter. Why clarify? Because for any sautéing or for cooking crêpes or pancakes, or other uses such as greasing a cake pan, it butters better and lessens the chance of sticking, and, without its solids, the butter is much less likely to burn. Both aspects contribute to a better appearance of the "good" side of a crêpe or pancake.

To clarify, melt the butter over low heat in a heavy saucepan, and continue cooking for three to five minutes without stirring. Three layers will be formed: a top, thin layer of foam; the larger middle layer of clear, golden oil; and a lower layer of milky solids. Remove from heat, and allow to sit for 5 minutes.

Skim off the foam layer with a large spoon or a skimmer. Then gently, carefully, and slowly pour off the clear butter-oil into a clear container, trying not to disturb the bottom-layer solids. Discard the dregs. If you are uncertain of the pouring, or want to be positive that no residue gets into the clear butter, then strain it through a fine sieve lined with cheesecloth.

Stored in the refrigerator in a covered container, clarified butter will keep indefinitely; so while going to the trouble to clarify butter, do a large amount. When melted, clarified butter is handled and measured like an oil, but when refrigerated it solidifies and can be measured as a solid shortening. Clarifying butter reduces its volume by about one-fourth, thus two sticks of butter will yield about ¾ cup (18 cL).

## MELTING CHOCOLATE

Chocolate melts at about 90°F (32°C), and thus should be melted slowly and carefully over very low heat since it will scorch easily. The usual way is to place the chocolate into a bowl or other container which is set over hot, not boiling, water or into the top of a double boiler. If you are careful, you can melt chocolate over very low direct heat, *but* use a small pan (when the chocolate is melted, you do not want a thin layer), preferably a heavy or thick pan, and remove it from the heat before the chocolate has completely melted. The residual heat in the pan will finish the melting, which you can assist by stirring the partially melted chocolate. Coarsely chopping the chocolate helps speed the melting of the chocolate; you do not require as much heat to get to the center of those big pieces. Above all, be careful because chocolate burns easily.

Also, the pan for melting should be dry. You do not want to introduce small amounts of any liquid. Melting the chocolate and then blending it with larger amounts of liquid, however, does work satisfactorily. If your melting chocolate picks up a little bit of water and as a result turns tight, stiff, and lumpy, you can salvage the chocolate by stirring in 1 teaspoon (5 mL) of homogenized vegetable shortening per ounce of chocolate that you melted. Stir until smooth, and then forget that you have added the shortening; just proceed with the recipe. *Do not* add butter, which will have the effect of adding a bit more water to the water-caused problem.

## WORKING WITH EGG YOLKS

Egg yolks are a thickening agent for sauces, custards, and the like. Two large egg yolks offer the thickening effect of 1 tablespoon (9 g) of flour. However, in the preparation of such recipes, the egg yolks must be treated more carefully than flour. If they are to be beaten before adding to the other ingredients, pay attention to the descriptive term used, and beat only to that state.

If the egg yolks are to be heated, then be careful about the heat, for an egg yolk can scramble in a blend or batter, much as it would in a frying pan when you are fixing the morning breakfast. The heat source should be gentle or moderate and the sauce should be stirred constantly with a flat-edged spoon using a stirring pattern which scrapes all inside surfaces: bottom, side wall, and corners. If you are to add the egg yolks while heating the sauce, then add them one at a time, stirring the whole time to minimize the chance of curdling.

If an egg-yolk mixture is to be added to a hot sauce, remove a small amount of the sauce from the saucepan and stir it into the egg yolks. Then add this warmed, diluted egg-yolk mixture to the saucepan, and stir constantly until the sauce is thickened.

## BEATING EGG WHITES

The egg whites and the bowl must be free from all fat of any nature, which includes any trace of egg yolk. If, when separating the eggs, a bit of yolk falls in with the white, then you might be able to retrieve it with the aid of a piece of egg shell, or use a kitchen baster to suck up the bit of yolk along with a small amount of the white.

Do not beat egg whites in a plastic bowl, for plastic tends to absorb and retain fat once it has been placed in the bowl. Do not use an aluminum bowl, for a chemical reaction can give a grayish cast to the whites. Do use a copper bowl and a large balloon whisk to beat the whites by hand, if you want to use the only true way to beat egg whites. If you are using this approach, then the copper bowl should be cleaned before each use with a mixture of salt and either lemon juice or vinegar to remove any oxidation, grease, or fat. Such a bowl should never, never be cleaned with soap, because soap is part fat.

Copper bowls may be "best," but stainless-steel or other metal ones will also yield very good results. Glass or porcelain are also very good, but there is a bit of argument that their sides are slippery and thus not an optimal surface to hold the beaten whites. Adding a small amount of cream of tartar and a small amount of salt to the beating egg whites give a bit of acidity and a chemical reaction to enhance the stabilization of the air-filled whites, thus helping the whites hold their volume. The cream of tartar should be used unless you are beating the whites in a copper bowl; under that circumstance the cream of tartar and the copper will combine chemically to give a greenish cast to the whites.

However much it is argued that hand beating is best, realism says that most of us will use an electric mixer to beat egg whites. Therefore it is important to keep all of the whites in motion while beating, and thus you should use the smallest bowl which will serve your need. If the beaters and bowl are stationary, use a spatula to keep all of the egg whites coming into the path of the beaters. If you are using a hand-held portable mixer, move the beaters all around the inside of the bowl.

Have the egg whites at least at room temperature, or slightly warmer, to beat optimally. The beaters should also be at room temperature. Start beating rather slowly until the whites begin to foam, whether beating by hand or by machine. Add the small amounts of cream of tartar and salt, and then gradually increase the speed of the beating action to fast. Keep all of the whites in motion, and beat in as much air as possible until the whites reach their desired state. Beating may, if you desire, be finished off by hand. And finally, having a bit of sugar in the beaten whites, even diverting some if the recipe does not call for any in the whites, helps one better judge the current state of beating.

To judge the appearance of the whites, check for the following situations:

*Foamy:* large uneven air bubbles are apparent.

*Begins to hold shape:* fine, close-together air bubbles, a white appearance; lifting the beaters will leave a mark.

*Soft peaks:* the whites form peaks, but the tips will bend over.

*Stiff but not dry:* defined, sharp peaks will hold their point; the whites are a uniform white color with a glistening appearance.

*Stiff and dry:* the peaks are still stiff, but the appearance has gone past white to speckled and dull, powdery and granular; whites beaten to this state will not rise when heated, nor will they last long.

And for some final, brief comments on egg whites:

- Eggs that are at least a week old will beat up better than fresh eggs.
- Use your egg whites as soon as you can after they have been beaten. If the whites have been folded into a batter, that does not mean that the batter can be held; it should be baked or whatever as soon as practical.
- Egg whites may be folded into either a warm or a cold sauce or batter, unlike whipped cream which melts when exposed to warmth.
- See the comments on eggs (page 26) and on folding (page 20).

**WHIPPING CREAM**

Have the cream and your equipment chilled. If the kitchen is very warm, then set the bowl in a larger bowl which contains a layer of ice and water.

To whip cream by hand, use a large, chilled metal (but not copper) bowl and a chilled large, balloon-type whisk, made with thin, flexible wires. Whip the cream, keeping it all in motion, until it reaches the desired state of doneness.

To whip by electric mixer, work with a chilled bowl and chilled beaters (a whisk-type beater is even better). Start beating at a slow speed and gradually increase the mixing speed to medium-high or high, the latter with small amounts of cream. Lift the beaters as appropriate to incorporate as much air as possible into the cream. If the bowl revolves on its stand, use a spatula as needed to keep all of the cream in motion and flowing into the beaters. If you are using a hand mixer, move the beaters around the bowl so that all of the cream is in motion and being whipped evenly at the same time.

To whip by food processor, chill the cream and equipment. Since the food processor will not incorporate as much air into the whipped cream, watch carefully to see that you do not overwhip.

An optional strategem if you whip with a machine is to stop just short of the desired state of doneness, and finish off the whipping by hand. Any large whisk can be used, and there is less risk of overbeating.

Unlike egg whites, whipped cream can have the sugar and any flavoring added at the beginning of the whipping operation. However, later addition of those ingredients may let the whipping go faster.

You can judge your whipping progress by checking for the following situations:

*Begins to thicken:* a thick, custardlike consistency.

*Soft peaks or holds its shape:* whisk or beaters leave marks when removed from the cream, and soft peaks are held. A bit of cream lifted and dropped will softly retain its shape.

*Stiff:* beat slightly longer, until the cream is a bit stiffer and forms definite peaks which are not as sharp and stiff as the ones formed by beaten egg whites.

*Butter:* the "woops" state from which there is no recovery, just enjoyment of the resulting product.

A variety of factors affect how cream behaves when whipped. Since the time between states can be a matter of seconds, once the cream finally begins to thicken noticeably, you should watch it carefully.

If you have whipped the cream before you want to serve it, cover and refrigerate until serving time. I have enjoyed whipped cream more than a day later. At the last moment, check the whipped cream which probably has separated slightly and may have a watery bottom. Reincorporate the liquid, and freshen the cream by beating it briefly with a wire whisk. Alternately, set the whipped cream in a fine-mesh sieve, which is set into a bowl, and let the liquid drip into the bowl.

And for some final, brief comments on whipping cream:

- To sweeten whipped cream always use confectioners' sugar. Granulated sugar will melt, as will particles of crushed candy, leading to a rather strange consistency for the whipped cream.
- Beating the cream improperly or too fast at the beginning can cause the butterfat in the cream to separate more quickly. This makes the whipped cream less airy, less stable, and more likely to melt.
- Whipped cream liquifies when it comes in contact with hot ingredients, thus when it is folded into a dessert, the other ingredients should be cold. Obviously, it should only top a cold dessert.
- You can stretch your whipped cream, and have a lower calorie product, if you fold a stiffly beaten egg white into 1 cup (24 cL) of cream which has been whipped.
- When *overwhipped,* cream separates before it becomes butter. Should this happen there is no recovery. Salvage something and just continue beating until you make butter, plain or with whatever flavorings you were incorporating into the cream. The butter made from cream was sweetened with confectioners' sugar and flavored with triple sec and it made for tasty and interesting toasted English muffins.

# Some Comments on Ingredients

**BUTTER**

Does unsalted — sweet — butter really make a difference? Yes, certainly in a purist sense, but not really if you cannot find the sweet butter, or if it is much more expensive than the regular salted butter.

Salt's original purpose in butter was as a preservative to help increase shelf life. The estimate is that there is about ½ teaspoon (3 g) of salt in a quarter-pound (115 g) stick of butter.

Salted and sweet butter are effectively interchangeable where cooking and flavor are concerned. The sweet (unsalted) butter with its shorter shelf life may be somewhat fresher than the salted butter which you might purchase at that same time, and that freshness element may make a difference; but there is no guarantee that sweet butter will always be fresher than the salted. Certainly if your recipe includes salt as one ingredient, there would seem to be little difference in a cooked product.

Margarine simulates butter and can be substituted, however it has neither the taste nor the texture of butter, and it has a higher melting point than butter. There are new blends — part butter and a larger part margarine — but I have not had any experience with them in baking.

As a final comment, the choice between the two butters may well depend on whether you should avoid salt in your diet.

**FLOUR**

The flour called for in these recipes for the most part is all-purpose flour, but occasionally cake flour. Since both types of flour are conventionally sold in the United States as presifted — sifted before packaging and somewhat settled during shipment and handling — no further sifting is required prior to measurement. Dip your measure into the flour, lift it out, and level it off with a straight edge.

If you want to sift the flour first and then measure it, you should add an additional half of the measure called for in the recipe; that is, if the recipe calls for 1 cup, you will need 1½ cups of the freshly sifted flour.

*Pink Squirrel Mousse Pie, pages 36-37 and 41*

## SUGAR AND OTHER SWEETENERS

In a number of the recipes you may want to experiment with substituting another sweetener for sugar. To that end, the following may be tried:

*Honey:* ⅓ cup (70 g) granulated sugar = ⅓ cup (8 cL) honey, plus a pinch of baking soda. (Do not add the soda if sour cream or sour milk is used in the recipe.) Reduce the water by 1½ tablespoons (2 cL).

*Molasses:* ⅓ cup (70 g) granulated sugar = ⅓ cup (8 cL) molasses. (Omit any baking powder and add ½ teaspoon or 3 g baking soda.) Reduce the water by 1 tablespoon (15 mL).

*Dark corn syrup:* ⅓ cup (70 g) granulated sugar = ⅓ cup (8 cL) dark corn syrup. Reduce the water by 1 tablespoon (15 mL).

*Maple syrup:* ⅓ cup (70 g) granulated sugar = ⅓ cup maple syrup plus 1 tablespoon (15 mL) white corn syrup. Reduce the water by 1½ tablespoons (2 cL).

For any such substitution, *if there is no water in the recipe* for you to reduce, add a generous tablespoon (12 g) of flour to that called for in the recipe.

If by chance you are out of brown sugar, and do have unsulphured molasses, you can substitute ¼ cup (25 g) granulated sugar plus 1 tablespoon (15 mL) unsulphured molasses for ¼ cup (25 g) brown sugar. Or 1 cup (195 g) brown sugar and be replaced by 1 cup (205 g) granulated sugar plus ¼ cup (6 cL) unsulphured molasses. No premixing is needed; just add the two ingredients at the place in the recipe which calls for the brown sugar.

A simple syrup is used in several recipes. It is an advance blending of sugar and water, and can be made in quantity. It stores easily and well, for the sugar stays in suspension under refrigeration, and even reasonably well at room temperature. The simple syrup can be made in any desired level of sweetness:

> *2 parts sugar + 1 part water   =   2 parts simple syrup*
> *2 parts sugar + 2 parts water  =   3 parts simple syrup*
> *1 part sugar  + 2 parts water  = 2½ parts simple syrup*

The easiest measure or part to use is a cup, but any volume measure is possible. Place the sugar and water in a saucepan, stir to dissolve the sugar, and bring the combination to a boil. Gently boil for five minutes. Remove from the heat and pour into a large bowl to cool; transfer to a storage jar.